IMAGES OF ENGLAND

# Around
# Northallerton

Eileen Gaskell in motor patrol uniform, 1940s. She was a member of the Women's Auxiliary Police Corps, formed in 1941 as part of war-time National Service and disbanded in 1946. It paved the way for the appointment of women to the regular police force. Only twelve of the eighty Women Auxiliaries in the North Riding became drivers in the Motor Patrol Unit.

IMAGES OF ENGLAND

# Around Northallerton

Vera Chapman

NONSUCH

The Festival of Britain, 1951. Detail of a picture on page 74.

First published 1994
This new pocket edition 2005
Images unchanged from first edition

Nonsuch Publishing Limited
The Mill, Brimscombe Port,
Stroud, Gloucestershire, GL5 2QG
www.nonsuch-publishing.com

British Library Cataloguing in Publication Data.
A catalogue record for this book is available from the British Library.

ISBN 1-84588-176-1

Typesetting and origination by Nonsuch Publishing Limited
Printed in Great Britain by Oaklands Book Services Limited

# Contents

*DEDICATION*

*To the People of Northallerton*

# Introduction

This collection of around 220 old photographs is a personal portrait of Northallerton, a thriving market town and administrative centre of ancient origin, and the nucleus of a prosperous farming region. The County Town of North Yorkshire and formerly of the North Riding, it emerges as a town with a distinct personality, and a happy place to be.

This book is dedicated to the people of Northallerton. On them it focuses, in their many activities at work and at play. Numerous townspeople, and villagers too, have risen to the occasion and allowed me to copy their private and family photographs, and given of their time to discuss and interpret them. Without them this book would not exist.

The photographs range from the 19th century to the 1950s and a little beyond. The 1950s are especially well represented. Readers will be able to recognise themselves, their relatives and friends, and many people who have played a part in the life of the town. They are now on record in this, a memorial and a tribute.

Northallerton was "Aelfere's tun", Alfred's farm, and became a Saxon borough and centre of the Wapentake of Allerton. The prefix "North" distinguished it from other Allertons in Yorkshire. Its situation on the road between London and Edinburgh brought trade and visitors, but also death and destruction. The Saxon church and borough were ravaged in William the Conqueror's terrible Harrying of the North in 1069-70. The Norman church and borough survived the Scottish incursions repulsed nearby in 1138 at the Battle of the Standard. They did, however, suffer destruction by the Scots in the fourteenth century after the Battle of Bannockburn.

Allertonshire had been granted after the Norman Conquest to the Bishop of Durham. A short-lived motte and bailey castle followed by a Bishop's Palace were built near Northallerton's church. Neither was to survive, except as earthworks around the town's Victorian cemetery. Two medieval hospitals and two Friaries were founded and later disappeared. The site of the Carmelite Friary became the Friarage Hospital.

The Norman town developed southward as a planned extension, thereby creating a market place along the High Street. Its regular series of burgage plots ending in back lanes were later built over as densely populated yards, largely demolished in the 1950s. The first market charter was granted in 1200 AD and a limited Wednesday market in 1555. By the late eighteenth century the weekly Wednesday market was a feature, as now, throughout the year. Two annual fairs granted in 1200 AD had grown by the seventeenth century into four. By the nineteenth century, two remained as important fairs for the sale of cattle and horses. But droving ended when the railway came, and a Livestock Mart was set up by the station. Even so, animals were traded in the High Street until the end of the century. Now they assemble at the Applegarth Mart behind the High Street. The May Fair, however, is still an important recreative event.

In the eighteenth century, Northallerton's High Street was prospering as a market place and a staging point on the Great North Road. It also benefitted from being, from 1745, part of the Boroughbridge to Durham Turnpike Road. Four coaching inns flourished in the High Street, and by the nineteenth century there were around twenty inns or hotels. This prosperity is still reflected in the Georgian frontages above the present shops. Some facades represent new buildings, whilst others may have been the refronting of older properties.

The arrival of the Great North of England Railway in 1841, followed by rail links to London and Edinburgh and then to Stockton and to Hawes, drew development to the south and west of the town. South Parade from around 1860 gave direct access to the station. The town's central position continued to be important, shown by the building of the Court House, Prison, Registry of Deeds, and Police Headquarters. In 1873, a new Town and Market Hall came, and a cottage hospital was begun in 1877. From 1889, the North Riding County Council was formed, to be centered from 1906 at the splendid new County Hall on the former racecourse. From 1974, it continued as North Yorkshire County Council's County Hall. The town itself had become an Urban District with its own Council, and is now within Hambleton District. The ancient Grammar School, founded before 1323, gained a new site and buildings in 1909. The H.Q. of the 4th Battalion The Green Howards, Alexandra Princess of Wales's Own Yorkshire Regiment, was built on Thirsk Road. From a World War II emergency hospital the Northallerton group of hospitals developed. A new Northallerton Library building has recently been added next to the County Library Headquarters. After Local Government reorganisation in 1974, Hambleton District Council built its Civic Centre and a Community and Leisure Centre in the town.

Developments new and old recognise and reinforce the centrality of Northallerton. They attract people to the expanding town and enliven its life. They form the backcloth to the multifarious activities of Northallerton people past and present.

## One

# High Street, Market Place and Family Businesses

High Street, northward from Church Green, early twentieth century.

High Street, c. 1950s. Mrs D. Hardisty remembers seven little cottages and a stream in the yard where Nelson's electrical shop now is.

The Buck Inn. Near the old Grammar School and parish church, the inn is little changed apart from its sign, which announced Tower Ales, Tadcaster. The man posing in front may be the proprietor. To the left was a sweetshop.

View from the parish church tower, 23 october 1952. Kellett and Pick's garage with old style petrol pumps has now gone from its site next to the Methodist church. (*Ackrill Newspapers Ltd*)

The Central Cinema in the 1950s. It was demolished to make a road from the roundabout into the Applegarth car park. (Miss Edna Sedgwick)

High Street and Town Hall. Built in 1872-3 on the site of the old shambles, the Town Hall was designed by John Ross of Darlington, "one of the most eminent architects in the North". Mrs Dorothy Hardisty recalls that its ground floor used to house a butcher's, a sweetshop and a hairdresser's. The row on the left included Ankers, Fairburn the chemist, McNally's cake shop and Law's clothing shop. On the right was Miss Russell's cafe.

Market place. Fairs were held from about 1200 AD. The Wednesday market is first mentioned in 1334, but is probably much older. It is still a popular attraction on this part of High Street, but farm animals are traded at Applegarth Mart. The Golden Lion, built about 1730, was a staging post on the Great North Road, with extensive stabling. Now a hotel, it is a venue for social occasions. Reach for the Stars, with Kenneth More, was filmed here. Sam Turner's market stall spread over the slope in front.

*Right:* Shoppers at High Street market stall, 1950s. (Miss Edna Sedgwick)

*Below: Left:* market day, 1950s. The Black Bull is on the left.

*Left:* A yard behind High Street, 1950s. This was possibly Barker's Yard, now Market Row. (Miss Edna Sedgwick)

*Below:* Bull yard, c. 1950s. These houses stood behind the Black Bull Inn. Bull Yard ended at East Road, formerly called Back Lane.

*Above:* another High Street yard, 1950s. (Miss Edna Sedgwick)

*Right:* Northallerton yard, 1950s. The regular pattern of yards ending in a back lane at Applegarth and at East Road was probably laid out in the Middle Ages, when the market was granted and Northallerton expanded from the old settlement around the parish church, the green and the Bishop's Castle and Palace.

South Parade.

Grammar School.

County Hall.

The Cross.

Parish Church.

Drill Hall

Market Place.

Northallerton.

Other notable town scenes.

Kellett and Pick. Their garage stood next to the Methodist church, and the premises are now an estate agency. The firm also had two other businesses in town, the Metropole showrooms and the Ainderby Road garage and showrooms. (Miss Edna Sedgwick)

J. Cleminson, ironmonger, 1888. John Cleminson founded the firm in 1886 near the Town Hall. His daughter, Miss May Cleminson, continued the business until she died in 1966, leaving it to her three full-time staff who carried it on. Eventually the two older staff retired, and Mr B. Holmes continues it in partnership with his brother. In the 1960s there were four hardware shops in town; now there is only this one. An iron wringer in the shop has the Cleminson name on it. James Guthrie, a currier, traded next door on the left.

A poster, 1889. This announced that J. Cleminson had taken the oldest established ironmongery business in the town, carried on successfully by Mr Richard Taylor for thirty-two years. The photograph above shows a similar range of stock, with wooden rakes and scythe handles prominent.

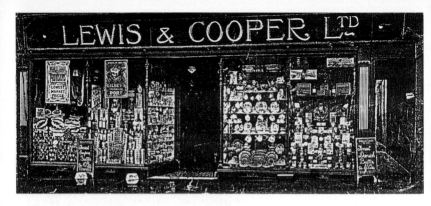

## GOOD NEWS
## ANOTHER REDUCTION !

In the price of Hams and Bacon. After the high prices ruling throughout the winter, it is indeed welcome news to the Housewife. We are offering the very finest quality of Hams and Bacon cheaper than ever, and we want everybody to know it.

**FINEST
MILD
CURED**

# HAMS

**EVERY HAM
WARRANTED
PERFECTION.**

They are selected from the finest young farm-fed Pigs and weigh about 12lbs. to 14lbs. The bones are small and there is scarcely an atom of waste. They are mild and lean and of the most delicious flavour and the price is now only

**Satisfaction Guaranteed,
or Money refunded.**

## 7d. per lb.

**You cannot buy better
whatever price you pay.**

They are salt-cured in the old fashioned way, and many of our customers who have tried them, have said, "**like the last,**" it was perfection : that speaks for itself, doesn't it ? We are not spending money in advertising second or third rate brands. **We know** we have a good article to offer which is both **cheap and good.**

We are now also able to offer the very best prime

**ALL the bones taken out.
Easy to Slice.
No Loss or Waste.**

## MILD CURED
## ROLL BACON

Being salt-cured it will keep.
The fat and lean are nicely blended.
Try it, it will please you.

If you take a whole Roll which only weighs about 30lbs. we can charge

You can have half a Roll either end, at halfpenny per lb. more. Never been known so cheap.

## 6½d. per lb.

Try a few pounds in slices at 7½d. per lb. You can then buy a piece if you are pleased with the quality.

We have reduced the price of Bacon all round and we can offer, if you take a side,

## CUMBERLAND CUT
## MILD CURED BACON 6d. per lb.

We cut any size piece at slightly increased prices, and we give a Bonus of 1/- in the £ on all Cash Purchases of provisions.

# LEWIS & COOPER, LTD.,
## NORTHALLERTON.

*Above:* Lewis and Cooper, 1933. Photographed for Town and Country News, the business had then been established for more than a century, trading, as now, in china and glassware, wines, spirits and groceries. Farmhouse hams and Wensleydale cheese were sent to all parts of Britain and abroad. Mr F. Bell, the then manager, had twenty-one employees. The two boards on the pavement offer Finest Empire Butter at 10d per lb. and Finest Danish Butter at 1s 1d per lb.

*Left:* Hams and bacon. This advertisement appeared in the *Northallerton, Romanby* and *Deighton Parish Magazine*, April 1908.

*Right:* China and glass. In the same *Parish Magazine,* May 1908, we are told that china and glass could be repaired no matter into how many pieces it was broken!

*Below:* The co-op, 1927. Staff were, front row, left to right: E. Pepperday, C. Pollard, L. Colley, J. Willoughby, M. Burley, H. Brown, G. Finkill, P. Ward, H. Wright. At the rear: A Weighell, J. Brown and L. Weighell.

The second shop front. It was altered again later and the business sold after the Hirds had traded there for seventy-five years. George Hird founded his firm of pharmaceutical chemists in 1908 in the former premises of J.H. Porter, tailor and outfitter. George (see page 72) was a Liberal campaigner and active in many organisations, including the Cricket Club. His son, Kenneth, a captain in the Green Howards attached to the Indian Army, joined the business in 1948, played for the Cricket Club, and was a U.D. Councillor and Chairman of the Chamber of Trade. Walter Willson, a northern group of grocery stores, was next door.

T. Smirthwaite's garage. Now refronted as Argos, Tom Smirthwaite's business continues at the rear in East Road. His first garage was in Romanby Road. Next door on the left, the fresh fish shop of J.H. Harrison is continued under the same name by Ron Jones. (Miss Edna Sedgwick)

*Right:* Mr Dennis and Mr Parry, 1933. Arthur Dennis, on the left, whose father was also a shoemaker, began the business in Zetland Street *c.* 1880 with a boy assistant. In 1923, David Parry invested in the business and new machinery was put in. Apprentices still had to learn to make boots and shoes by hand, however, serving a 4-5 years apprenticeship for £1 15s per week. When qualified, this increased to £2 10s. Dennis and Parry employed two men and six apprentices, but themselves took only £3 10s per week.

*Below:* The Boot and Shoe repairing factory. The premises have changed little in appearance. Arthur Dennis is on the left.

Workroom in the shoe factory, 1933. (*Town and Country News*, 19 May 1933.) Alan Grainger has recently taken on the business with his son. Pam still does hand repairs.

The mineral water factory, 1927, now demolished. The firm was established on the medieval Friarage site in 1878. Soda Water and Dry Ginger were a speciality. The small building to the left was the mortuary. "No interference from there," says Mr Swain.

Mineral water factory interior, early 1930s. Jack Swain is at the vat. Soda water and essences were the ingredients.

Mineral water factory interior, early 1930s. George Espiner is at the pipes.

*Above:* A decorating business. Frank Myers set up his business in 1910 at Fir Tree House in Leeming village. During the Great War he did Government work (D.C.R.E.). The photograph was probably taken at about that time. His was the only car and telephone in the village, and he recalled playing cricket along the A1. The family then moved to Northallerton, and his son Leslie and his wife played an active part in town life.

*Left:* David Nesbit, of Ashwell Nesbit, heating engineers, Leicester, installed the heating system into County Hall when it was built *c.* 1906. He was a cousin of Elizabeth Hay, wife of W.G. Hay, the South Parade grocer.

W.G. Hay's grocery, south parade. William Gowan Hay, centre, grandfather of Gowan Swain, bought an existing business c. 1902. South Parade had been made in the 1860s, to improve access to the station. The shop is now the Voluntary Services Bureau.

Thomas Hay. W.G. Hay's brother Thomas had a flour mill by the railway at North End, where Great Mills now is. He owned a large house, Ashlands, on Bullamoor Road.

T. Places's men leading timber. Horses as used here were ousted by mechanical traction. Since the Second World War horses have been found useful on soft ground and difficult terrain for timber haulage on the flanks of the North York Moors.

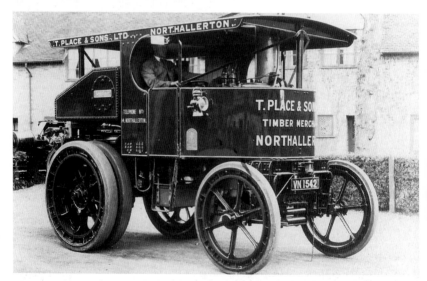

T. Place and sons ltd steam haulage tractor, c. 1920s. The water tank and drum for winding haulage ropes can be seen at the rear. There is an oil lamp, a mirror and a number plate for use on roads. The "driver" is wearing a suit, not working clothes, and may be posing for the delivery of the shiny new vehicle. Thomas Place became an alderman of the town.

*Right:* Grandma Crow. Her son Sam founded the Crow family firm which lives and over-winters its fairground equipment beside the Applegarth.

*Below:* A Crow Roundabout at Leyburn October fair, *c.* 1912. Ripon was the next stop. Sam Crow played in Milburn's Brass Band in Middlesbrough and founded his fairground firm there. When the Second World War came, the War Agricultural Executive Committee asked him to operate engines for threshing in the area. There was one available in Northallerton. He bought it, and from 1940 the Crows have been based in the town. Whilst feeding the horses in Darlington, Sam himself was kicked and killed by one.

Fairman's engine, 1936. S. Crow and Sons' Burrell Showman's Engine, No. 3872, Hero, at the Hoppings Fair on Newcastle Town Moor, 25 June 1936. Grandsons now follow in the business, in which mechanical expertise is important.

Threshing during the Second World War. Sam Crow and son Billy stand beside the machine near Northallerton.

International tractor. A cab was put on to the tractor during the Second World War, a forerunner of post-war legislation to reduce farm accidents. Billy Crow leans against the rear.

Emergency work, 1942. When a farmer's threshing machine broke down, he paid Billy Crow extra to haul his machine up a very steep hill in the Kirby Knowl, Knayton, area and down again. Billy is on the right, and Ernie Rowland of Borrowby is next to him.

Something to Crow about. "All British", "Uncle Sam" and "Something to Crow About" are some of the slogans on the scrolls on Crow's Thriller. Stanley Crow is on the right of the four men. A similar roundabout, Crow's Waltzer, appeared at Barnard Castle Meet in 1994.

Fairground organ. Tim Ray's Gallopers Organ, ex-Corrigan's, at Woburn Rally, 1958, was admired by the Crows.

## Two

# Churches and Schools

The old vicarage.

The parish church of all saints' and High Street. This south-east view shows the Georgian chancel built in 1779. Earlier steep roof marks can be seen on the tower. The chancel was again rebuilt during the Victorian restoration of 1884 by C. Hodgson Fowler.

The parish church from the south west. The vast roof spanning nave and aisles replaced three separate lead-covered roofs in 1787. The nave and transepts were given steep roofs again in the 1884 restoration.

*Right:* The Revd Thomas Warren Mercer, M.A.
He was the Vicar from 1849 to 1876.

*Below:* The parish church choir. This choir won
the first prize in the Swaledale Tournament of
Song in 1903 and 1905.

The Revd Frederick Talbot Baines, M.A. He was the Vicar from 1935 to 1951.

The Revd S.S. Thistlewood, M.A. He was the Vicar from 1951 to 1962.

Zion congregational church, c. 1860. The earliest group of Sunday School teachers photographed with the Revd Thomas Yeo, Pastor 1853-1865. They were Richard Hardwick, Miss Airton, George Dowson, Miss Margaret Tesseyman, Miss Rebecca Robinson, Thomas Trotter, Miss Hamilton, Miss Mary Dowson, Miss Ayre, the Revd Thomas Yeo, Miss J.A. Dowson, Miss Small, Farrow Vasey, George Ayre and J. Torr Robinson.

Zion sunday school teachers, 1880. The church was built in 1818 after services had been held from the late 18th century at the Market Cross and in cottages. It became Northallerton United Reformed Church in 1972. The Sunday School was built in 1858 on a plot of land reserved for a burial ground extension before the town cemetery was opened.

Zion sunday school officers and teachers, 1918. The Pastor, the Revd Fred J.R. Young, stands at the centre back.

Zion young men's mutual improvement society, 1918. The Society was founded in 1880, when the Revd J.W. Parsons was Pastor and Chairman. It had a Bible Society, a Debating Society and a room for reading and games. Football (see page 48), gymnastics, tennis, cricket, cycling, debates, competitions, social gatherings and lectures took place.

*Right:* The revd fred j.r. young. He was the Pastor at Zion from 1904 to 1920.

*Below:* Trial by jury, 30-31 march 1927. Zion choir and friends performed Gilbert and Sullivan in the church hall. Mrs P. Parker's mother, then Mary (Mollie) Simpson, aged 16, was one of the singers. She was a waitress at Miss Russell's cafe near the Town Hall. On marriage to Herbert Rudd, a skilled thatcher, she lived at Kirby Sigston, and put chickens on the train for transport. Herbert won many garden produce prizes at Osmotherley Show, and at the North Yorkshire Show won the Webb (Seeds) Master Gardener Plaque for 1979.

A Salvation Army wedding, 1927. William Lewis and Janet Fleming were Captains serving in Northallerton in the 1930s, and retired here in 1965. They lived to be 87 and 92 respectively, and celebrated their Diamond Wedding, by which time they had five children, thirteen grandchildren and thirteen great grandchildren.

William (Pop) Lewis. Again he is in Salvation Army uniform. After retirement, Lewis served as an Independent on Northallerton Urban District Council, and campaigned vigorously to Save the Hospitals, Save the Applegarth and Save the Town Hall. He also served on Hambleton District Council.

William (Pop) Lewis and the band, 1937. Lewis's father was a military bandsman. William enlisted in the First World War as a Royal Marine Bandsman, served on HMS *Concord*, and helped refugees during the Russian Revolution. From 1921 he served in the Salvation Army, but returned to the Royal Navy in the Second World War. Settling in Northallerton, he re-formed the Town Band, began the annual Brass Band Festival, taught many local children to play, and campaigned against Purchase Tax on Brass Band instruments. He also played a rare instrument, the cornopean, hand-made in 1832, a predecessor of the cornet.

Cauton house school.

West House School, *c.* 1913. Mrs Alderson's school near Applegarth Mart was earlier run by a son of the Revd Samuel Jackson, Zion Pastor 1848-49. Children from well-known firms include Eden greengrocers, Rooks greengrocers, Cleminson ironmongers and Pearson butchers. Back row, left to right: Agnes Bourne, May Smith, Bert Smith, Boy Eden, Leslie Bracewell, Wilf Barker, Charles Smith, Fred Thompson, Jack Swain, Emily Swain, Violet Cotton, Mrs Alderson. Centre row: May Pattison, Roland Pearson, ? Willoughby, Connie Hill, Dolly Lacey, Edna Bell, May Cleminson, ? Bertram, Olive Rooks, Evelyn Dale, Doris Milner, Mione ?. Seated, front row: Jack Tinsley, Muriel Forster, Harold Fisher, Billy Smith, Fred Willows, Jack Brigham, Digby Pearson, Millie Smith, Ivy Hill, teacher Doris ?. In front: John Rooks, Thompson Alderson, Leslie Benington.

Applegarth School infants, *c.* 1954.

The HMS *Hood* cups, 1940. Early in the Second World War, when Miss Weighell was the headteacher, Northallerton Primary School (now Applegarth County Primary School) adopted the battle cruiser HMS *Hood*, flagship of the Royal Navy, and sent "comforts" to the crew. On 27 February 1940, the crew presented two cups to the school. One is still awarded in inter-house sports competitions, the other to winners of a local football competition. In 1941, during the Battle of the Atlantic, HMS *Hood* was sunk when a shell from the Bismark hit the ship's magazine and the "Mighty Hood" spectacularly blew up. Of her crew of 1,418 men, fewer than a dozen survived. Subsequently the school adopted HMS *King George V*, and learned about the Neptune ceremony on crossing the Arctic Circle. This photograph was later presented to the school by Bill Childerstone, who was the little boy on the left. He attended the school from 1940 to 1945 and lived at the Golden Lion, where his parents were in management. The girl at the back was Enid Finkill.

Applegarth School first juniors, 1956. The teacher, Miss Rowntree, later became Mrs Swainston and Head of Infants at Richmond. On the back row, left hand end, is Brian Myers.

Staff, Applegarth School, 1956. Back row, left to right: Mrs Cowan, Mrs Swainston, Ethel Myers, Rosie ?. Front row: Kathleen ?, Miss Dorothea Lee, Mr Ralph Oliver, headmaster, -?-, -?-.

Applegarth children, *c.* 1956. The teacher is Mrs Myers.

Staff, Applegarth School, 1960. Back row, left to right: Mrs Elsie Ansell, clerk, Mrs Ethel Myers, Mrs Freda Jennings, Miss Doreen Wise. Front row: Mrs Elaine Parrington, Miss Dorothea Lee, Mr Ralph Oliver, headmaster, Mrs Muriel Cowan, Miss Audrey Helm.

Schools kitchen staff, 1955. Photographed at the Central Kitchens, Romanby Road, now Kingdom Hall, are Mrs Smith, Miss Elsie Parrish, Mrs Glasper and Mrs Kathleen Eyles.

Kitchen staff, 1965. These ladies were the first to move into the Applegarth School kitchens. Mrs Terry, Miss Elsie Parrish, Mrs Glasper, Mrs Nelson and Mrs Dunn.

Library lesson period, 1951. Allertonshire County Modern School opened in Brompton Road in 1941-42. The teacher here is Miss Holliday. Seated, left to right: -?-, Moira Weighell, Shirley Robinson, Margaret Harker, Veronica Kirby, Joan Mason, Dorothy Wilde, Shirley Reid. Standing: Margaret Foster and Phyllida (Phyll) Warren.

Speech day, c. 1951. The headmaster, Mr N.C. Bryning, presides with prizewinners at Allertonshire Modern School. Phyllida Joy (née Warren) remembers back row, left to right: first Ann Kirby, fifth Betty Smith. Middle row: first Ray Moody, first girl Dorothy Wilde. Front row: Phyllida Warren, Shirley Reid, Betty Turnbull. Mr Bryning, now retired, attended the Golden Jubilee celebrations in 1991-92, when commemorative mugs were issued. The school is now Allertonshire School.

Northallerton Grammar School, 1937. This is the centre part of a long school photograph, taken in the Coronation Year of King George VI. Mr H.T. Palmer, second left, was the headmaster from 1921 to 1943.

Northallerton Grammar School, October 1962. An extract from another long photograph shows the headmaster, Mr A.T. Richardson, centre. The Grammar School was founded prior to 1323 on a site near the parish church. It opened on the site in Grammar School Lane in 1909. About 1975 it became a Comprehensive School, and is now Northallerton College for all over 14 years of age, and includes adult education.

# Three

# Sport and Leisure

The Buck Inn darts team, 1947-48. Back row, left to right: George Lancaster, Jack Hutchinson, Wilf Terry, Kit Johnson, Eric Hanson, Tot Featonby. Front row: Alec Jack, Bill Grainger, Geoff Wetherall, Ivan Paley, Jack Johnson (landlord), Alf Glover.

Quoits club team, Nags Head Inn.

Mutual Football team, Zion Congregational church, 1890-91.

Northallerton Borough Band, 1875. It won the second prize in the Darlington Silver Band Competition. Back row, left to right: T. Jenkinson, H. Doughty, A. Barker, J. Barker, E. Thompson, E. Stockhill, T. Fowler, R. Weighell. Front row: J. Meynell, C. Fowler, H. Lumley, G. Curry, J. Barnett, P. Neal, R. Shuttleworth.

Romanby Football Club Team, 1903-4. It won the Allertonshire League Elliott Bowl and the Milbank Cup. Back row, left to right: T. Wilson, T. Thompson, J. Todd, T. Castle, J. Wilson, G. Castle, J. Gibson. Middle row: T. Wilson, W. Waites, W. Wilson, J. Bagley. Front row: C. Hogg, M. Hogg, J. Smith, H. Mawson, W. Jones.

A village cricket team. Is it Otterington or Ainderby?

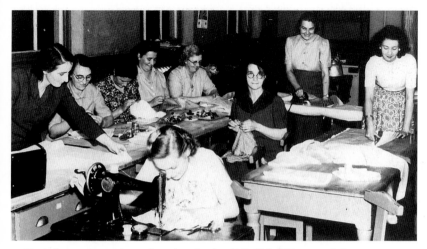

Northallerton evening dressmaking class, October 1949. (*Ackrill Newspapers Ltd*)

Northallerton Camera Club, 1950s. From the back, left to right: McCombie Metcalf, Mr Neasham, Harry Wright, -?-, Jack Suttill, Peter Blackey, ? Milne (with specs), Ron Jones, Geoff Naylor (at right hand side), Mrs Neasham, Miss Marchant, Mrs McCombie Metcalf, Arthur Elliott, Louis Oakley, -?-, Bill Greer (with moustache, a policeman), Joan Naylor, Mrs Harry Wright (at front).

Fire Service dinner at the golden lion, 1950s.

Fire Service children's party, 1950s.

County players at Northallerton Bowling Club, 27 september 1952. The Club House in the background, Fir Lodge, is now an Abbeyfield Home. The present Club House was built between Fir Lodge and the bowling green. The wooden pavilion at the corner of the green was moved bodily by crane on to the car park and is now the visitors' changing room.

Measuring from the jack, 1952. Whose bowl is nearest? The County players at the Club on 27 September.

Thirsk and Northallerton Golf Club. Leslie Myers, son of Frank Myers (page 24), is on the left.

Church House Badminton Club, 1957. Mr Holley is the winner; Miss Brown, a teacher at Allertonshire School, holds the other cup. Second from the right is Vernon Walters, who set up the firm Helix Springs in the old linoleum factory at North End in partnership with Mr Holley.

Northallerton Bowling Club, c. 1960s. For flat green bowling, the ladies had to dress smartly in white and wear hats. Ladies were allowed to play only in the afternoons until recently – at a lower membership fee. Mrs E.H. Stone, second from the right, won the Club's Singles Championship in 1961 and was runner-up in 1962. She became an All-England selector.

Northallerton Bowling Club triples championship, 1963. Left to right: C. Sorrell, E.H. Stone, M. Duggleby. Stone and Duggleby were also All-England Pairs semi-finalists in 1963.

Northallerton Motor Club, c. 1960. Left to right: Mrs Balfour, wife of Dr Balfour, partner with Dr Milne in their High Street practice, Leslie Myers and Mrs Ethel Myers. Rallies and Treasure Trails were club activities. Keith Schellenberg was a member. He later bought a Scottish island.

Northallerton Motor Club, 1960s. Awards were made for trails, driving and navigating by map references. Cup winners at the front are Mrs Myers and Miss Webster.

Some like it on foot, spring, 1964. The Chapman family, Ken, Timothy and Andrew, explore the footpath which became part of the Cleveland Way. A sprinkling of snow picks out a line of jet mine tailings on the front of the escarpment. Afforestation near Swainby and Scarth Nick has since obscured the adit mines where, in the Victorian heyday of jet jewellery, small partnerships of miners exploited the jet shales seam from the coastal cliffs to as far round as Osmotherley. (Vera Chapman)

Some like it on horseback, 1964. The Hurworth Hunt, which covers the Northallerton area, is seen here at the foot of the Cleveland Hills. (Mr Emerson Kirkup)

The Allertonshire Players, 1948. Moliere's *Le Bourgeois Gentilhomme* was presented in the Allerton Evening Institute. They also performed The Scoundrel Scapin.

*The Happiest Days of your Life*. Another performance by the Allertonshire Players included, left to right, Lee Vincent, Colin Bryson, John Rooke, Mary Ramsden, Barbara Charlton and Eileen Gaskell.

*The Shop at Sly Corner*, 1955, was also by the Allertonshire Players. Left to right: Valerie Wilkinson, Barry Cawthorne and William Robinson.

Northallerton Variety Company. This amateur company put on variety shows at Church House, Romanby Road. This and the next three photographs record shows in the early 1950s.

Northallerton Variety Company. Ron Jones can be recognised in two of these by his black moustache.

Northallerton Variety Company.

Northallerton Variety Company.

Pantomime *Cinderella*, 1955. Left to right are Cecil Richardson, Jeff Naylor, Terence Naylor, Gerald Asquith, Ron Jones and Dicky Wright.

A Scottish evening at the Golden Lion. On the left are four Scottish dancers, then, left to right: K.C. McKeown, Mrs and Dr McKenzie, -?-, -?-, Joan McKeown.

Whitsuntide Carnival and sports.

*Four*

# Special Occasions

"Cutting of the first sod of the Northallerton Water Works, 22 april 1892." Water was brought from springs at Thimbleby to service a reservoir at Bullamoor, completed in 1893, and pipes were laid in the town.

"Cutting the first sod of the Northallerton new Waterworks, 11 may l911. New sewage works were also made in 1911. The reservoir was completed in 1914.

"Turning the first sod, 13 December 1949". This was the Cod Beck reservoir on the moors above Osmotherley. It was built for the Northallerton and District Water Board (Chairman Councillor A.E. Skelton, JP), and opened in 1953. Despite progressive reservoir building, the expansion of the town and the still rising population of North Yorkshire mean a threat of water shortages in dry years, especially in the Dales.

*Right:* Queen Victoria's Golden Jubilee, 1887. This large poster announced a procession from noon, followed by a Meat Tea in four sittings in tents in the Market Place, followed by Sports on the RaceCourse. Northallerton Volunteer Band was to play selections. Meat was probably a luxury.

*Below:* "Patriotic gathering of 'the oddfellows' during the Boer War, 1899." This was outside the Oddfellows Arms near the parish church. The banner declares "United We Stand, Divided We Fall." The war ended in 1902. The signboard tells that J. Lazenby was "Licensed to Retail Ale Porter, Spiritous Liquors and Tobacco."

**NORTHALLERTON**
CELEBRATION OF THE JUBILEE OF HER MOST GRACIOUS MAJESTY QUEEN VICTORIA,
**On Tuesday, June 28th, 1887,**
Being the Fiftieth Anniversary of Her Majesty's Coronation.

PROGRAMME:
At TWELVE o'clock at Noon those intending to take part in the

**PROCESSION**
will assemble in the Town Street, near the Golden Lion Hotel, and will there be marshalled in the following order:—
VOLUNTEER BAND
VOLUNTEERS, under the command of Major Fowle
SCHOOL CHILDREN, under the direction of their respective Teachers
The BOROUGH BAILIFF and his Guests
MEMBERS OF THE JUBILEE COMMITTEE
FRIENDLY SOCIETIES.
GENERAL PUBLIC, mounted or on foot.

**A MEAT TEA**
Will be provided in TENTS in the MARKET PLACE,

AFTER THE TEA

**SPORTS**
and other Amusements will be provided on the RACE COURSE, kindly lent for the occasion by

The NORTHALLERTON VOLUNTEER BAND will play choice Selections of Music.

**GOD SAVE THE QUEEN!**

DAVID JACOB,
G. J. ROBINSON, } Hon. Secs.

Cyclists' meet, c. 1920.

An open air political meeting, 1920s. Mr C.B. Ord-Powlett MP addressing a crowd at Northallerton.

Roland (Roly) Walker's outing at bylands abbey, 1920s. A pub outing, this was one of the last horse-drawn journeys before motor coaches were adopted. S. and R. Walker ran a shared service between Northallerton and Brompton with Winn's. Today Winn Bros. and Abbott & Sons continue the shared service. Sid Walker died young, but Roly reached 70. Their father was known as "Toffee" Walker – he ran a sweetshop in Brompton!

Opposite: Visit of Princess Mary, july 1926. Town officials wait to greet the daughter of King George V and Queen Mary and wife of Viscount Lascelles, later Lord Harewood. As national Commandant of the Red Cross, her visit was to inspect some 800 North Riding members assembled on the cricket field beside County Hall. The Lascelles were amongst the chief landowners in Northallerton.

The Nags Head Inn, 5 may 1935, decorated ready for the following day's celebrations of the Silver Jubilee of King George V and Queen Mary.

Coronation of George VI and Queen Elizabeth, 1937. Lewis and Cooper celebrate with flag and bunting. This occasion followed the abdication of the uncrowned King Edward VIII.

Officers of the 4th battalion the Green Howards, 1941. The Green Howards (Alexandra, Princess of Wales's Own Yorkshire Regiment) were here photographed before they left for the Middle East. Colonel Littleboy is at the centre, front row. The 4th Battalion was a volunteer Territorial unit which recruited from the Northallerton, Thirsk, Richmond and Redcar areas. In peace time they normally all met together only at the annual camp.

Lieut-CoL. C.N. Littleboy, CB, DSO, MC, TD, DL. He was in command of the 4th Battalion, the Green Howards in the North Africa campaign during the Second World War.

Colonel Littleboy, seen here in later life.

Northallerton Branch, 4th battalion the Green Howards Annual Dinner, 1961. President Riorden, Col. of the Regiment, Brigadier G.E. Eden, Chairman Major Steel, Regimental Secretary Major Ibbetson. There were three Riordens in the Green Howards, all of whom were Regimental Sergeant Majors, and all were awarded the MBE.

March-past, 16 November 1950. The Chairman of the Council, J.L. Swain, and Town Officials stand in front of the Market Cross which has since been restored and repositioned farther along High Street. The occasion is probably the Armistice Day Parade.

Declaration of the poll, Town Hall, general election, 1951. Thomas Dugdale of Crathorne Hall was the Conservative MP for the Richmond Division of the North Riding 1929-59, and was a confidant of Prime Minister Stanley Baldwin during the abdication crisis of King Edward VIII. He was the Minister of Agriculture and Fisheries in Winston Churchill's government from 1951, a post for which his farming and landowning interests at Crathorne admirably suited him. On resignation in 1959, he was created first Baron Crathorne. He died in 1977. Left to right: Nancy Dugdale, Thomas L. Dugdale, Hubert Thornley, Richard Hoyle, Mrs Hoyle, Thomas and May Eustace Smith.

*Opposite above:* G.F. Hird presents the Council's Chain of Office to G.L. Swain. The ceremony took place in the Council Chamber. Mr Swain was a JP and member of the UDC and a County Councillor, and was awarded the MBE. He owned the Mineral Water Factory (see pages 22 and 23). Mr Hird began the pharmeceutical chemist's firm (see page 20). The site of his house on Thirsk Road is now a nursing home. (Ackrill Newspapers Ltd)

*Opposite below:* The Young Conservatives' bring and buy stall, September 1950. It was held in Northallerton Market Place.

The Festival of Britain, 1951. Celebrations were held on Church Green. Hospital patients enjoyed a front view from wheelchairs, prams, basket cots and mattresses. The detail on page 4 shows, behind the second cot from the left, Mrs Johnston, daughter Janet and Tom Johnston, County Veterinary Officer. But what were they watching? (Ackrill Newspapers Ltd)

*Opposite above:* The Proclamation of Her Majesty Queen Elizabeth II 1952. This followed the death of her father King George VI whilst she was in Kenya. In the photograph are Chairman UDC Councillor A.E. Skelton JP, and Councillors T.H. Lightfoot, C.F. Atkinson, J. Swain, A. Welsby, T. Jackson and R.C. Pick.

*Opposite below:* RAF Band's annual March-Past. That year the Mayor presided in High Street near the parish church. The town had close connections with RAF Leeming. In the background are The Buck Inn and the premises of Tom Willoughby, builder and plumber.

A doctor's wedding. At the wedding of Dr Mackay to Monica Smith, ward sister at the Rutson Hospital, doctors and their wives line up outside All Saints' parish church. Left to right: Mrs Wedderburn, Mrs Carter, Dr Carter, Dr Wedderburn, Mr McKeown, Mrs McKenzie, Mrs McKeown and Dr McKenzie.

"Miss Northallerton" Competition, early 1950s. (Miss Edna Sedgwick)

Red Cross toy collecting. The North Riding Branch collected toys for distribution. On the right is Eileen Gaskell.

Field day, Northallerton, 1950s. (Miss Edna Sedgwick)

Fire Service Christmas party, mid-1950s. Father Christmas is at the centre.

*Five*

# Hospitals, Doctors and Nurses

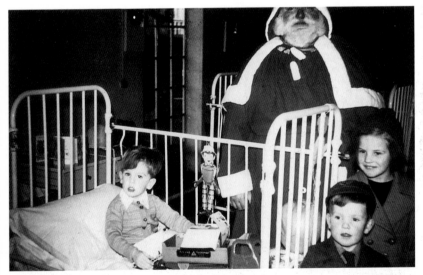

Santa visits Billy Banks, Friarage Hospital, Ward 10, 1955. Janet and William, Dr Edmunds' children, stand by. Each ward had a turkey and a doctor to carve it. Mr Albert Gaskell played Father Christmas for over twenty years at The Rutson, The Friarage and The Mount Hospitals.

*Left:* Henry Rutson, 1831-1920. A voluntary cottage hospital developed from 1877 in Vine House. In 1905, Henry Rutson of Newby Wiske donated this and adjacent property, thence known as The Rutson Hospital. It nursed servicemen in the First World War, and was an Emergency Station in the Second World War. In 1948 it became a National Health Service Hospital in the Northallerton Group.

*Below:* Vine House, the Rutson Hospital. The huge vine, possibly 200 years old, was a Black Hambro, and nicknamed the Bleeding Vine. An injury to its trunk "bled" until the flow was staunched by a gardener sent by the Duke of Northumberland, Sir Hugh Smithson, who was born in Northallerton.

Some Rutson nurses, 1977. Sister Green, Assistant Matron in charge of The Rutson, is seated second from the left.

Some Rutson staff and supporters, 1950s. At the rear, left, are Police Superintendant A.E. Clarke and Mr M. Wallace. The seated include Mrs Green, Mrs Rawlings and Mr John Weston Adamson, Chairman of the Management Committee for the Northallerton Group of Hospitals.

Cassy Harker. After being Matron at Chester, Miss Harker was Matron of the Friarage Hospital, Northallerton, 1952-63. She made it an important student nurse training centre, and a friendly place to be in. She then became Matron at Darlington Memorial Hospital until retirement. Her book Call Me Matron details from a personal viewpoint the changes in hospital practice during her career. In retirement she was an active Chairman of the Friends of Darlington Civic Theatre.

A.E. Clarke, MBE. "Nobby" Clarke, Chairman of the League of Friends of the Northallerton Hospitals 1957-83, was a great fund-raiser. Clarke House, which provides overnight accommodation for visitors to patients from outlying areas and to road accident cases, is named after him.

K.C. McKeown, CBE, DL, MCh, FRCS, FRCS (Edin). Mr McKeown was a much respected Senior Consultant Surgeon. He worked enthusiastically for the development of the Friarage Hospital from a collection of Second World War Canadian Army huts into a full-scale general hospital, and also for Darlington Memorial Hospital. He was elected a member and, later, the President of the Moynihan Society, the society for the nation's most eminent surgeons, and he and his specialist publications are of international influence.

A.W.B. Edmunds, MB, ChB, FRCP, FRCP (Edin), 1916-82. Born in China of Scottish parents, Dr Blair Edmunds served in the RAMC in East Africa, Ceylon and Burma. He became from 1952 a devoted Consultant Physician to the Friarage and Darlington Memorial Hospitals, living for ten years in Northallerton. In Darlington he developed the first coronary care unit in the Northern Region, and spent two years in the Government Health Service in Botswana. He died within a few months of retirement.

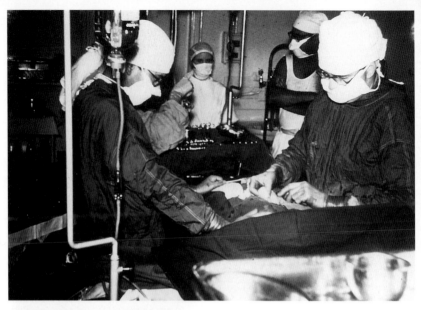

*Above*: A Friarage operation in progress. Performing it are Mr K.C. McKeown, right, and Mr Ganguli, now a professor in Canada.

*Left*: Sister Pearson.

*Opposite above*: An open day at the Friarage. Matron Harker encourages.

*Opposite below*: Staff group. Sister Dinsdale on the left moved to Glasgow and died young. The houseman was a doctor newly qualified after serving six months surgical and six months medical. Sister Tutor wears a maroon uniform. Sister Calvert, on the right, was in charge of the Women's Medical Ward. The verandah was an improvement to the row of detatched war-time emergency huts which long served as wards.

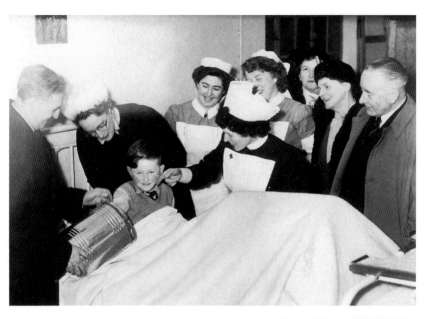

*Above:* Mrs Joan McKeown and sister F.M. Green MBE relax at a cocktail party. Sister Green was in charge at the Rutson Hospital from 1959.

*Left:* Dr Leslie Boyd was a Northallerton GP and partner of Dr McKenzie.

*Opposite above:* Sisters at a Christmas party, 1957. All were Yorkshire Dales girls and devoted staff members. Left to right: Sister Rhea, who was for long in charge of the Children's Ward, Sister Dinsdale, who managed the male medical ward, and Sister Calvert, who served the women's medical ward, and retired early.

*Opposite below:* the Friarage Hospital fête, june 1960. Left to right: Ward Sisters Gibson (surgical), Maddison (male medical) and McCabe 9 (medical) sell elderflower wine at stall W outside Ward 1. This was one of the original wooden huts of Oregon pine and cedarwood cladding from Canada erected in 1939-40 and still in use.

Hospital fête, June 1960. Punch and Judy delight the crowd.

Hospital Fête, June 1960. The band plays.

Nurses' graduation, 1950s. The ceremony was in one of the war-time emergency hospital huts which became an RAF Hospital from 1943-7 and were still in use as the eight wooden and eight brick wards of the Friarage Hospital established in 1948. Mr Weston Adamson is in the Chair, and Matron Harker, Mr McKeown and Mrs Constantine at the right hand end.

Nurses' graduation in the Town Hall. The spacious upper assembley room was used before the Recreation Hall was built at the Friarage. Back row, left to right: Dr Edmunds, Mrs Constantine, Dr McKenzie, Air Commadore Duck and Dr Owen. At the front is Gilbert Parker, an early male nurse.

Nurses' graduation, 1950s. This time the ceremony was in the new Recreation Hall, built after fund-raising and with Government grants. Hospital dances, nurses' pantomimes and social events were held there. At the rear is the Hospital Management Committee. Back row, left to right: Dr McKenzie, "Nobby" Clarke, -?-, -?-, and the Hospital Secretary. Front row: Dr Cameron, anaesthetist, Matron Harker, Mr Weston Adamson, Chairman, Mrs Weston Adamson, Sister Tutor and Dr Edmunds.

Prizewinners, 1957. The velvet curtains with fleurs-de-lys in the New Hall can be seen on either side. Most trainee nurses normally came from Wensleydale and Swaledale.

Prize day 1957. The speaker is Mrs Constantine. Left to right: Mr McKeown, Dr Owen, Matron Harker, Dr McKenzie, Sister Gibson and "Nobby" Clarke.

A hospital social event, c. 1953. Included are Mr and Mrs McKeown, Cassy Harker and Mr McKeown junior.

Doctors and their wives.

A skeleton, 1954. This was discovered in the grounds of the old Carmelite Friary from which the hospital took its name. The occasion was the building of old people's bungalows behind the Mineral Water Factory (page 22).

# Six

# The Early Railways and the Last Days of Steam

The railway comes to castle hills. An ancient encampment was enclosed into fields in the early 19th century. Much of the rest was levelled and the earth used to build the Great North of England Railway embankment in 1838-41. A Roman altar and coins were found at the time.

Northallerton Railway Station, 1845. The line from London to Darlington was opened in 1841, and completed to Gateshead in 1844. The Northallerton and Hawes Branch Railway opened in 1877, giving an impetus to quarrying in Wensleydale. It closed to passengers in the 1960s and to Redmire Quarries in 1993. The Stockton Branch Railway opened in 1854, and had a goods station at North End. Northallerton station buildings were demolished in 1987.

Railway Hotel, old livestock mart and racecourse. County Hall was built on the racecourse in 1902-6, and is reached via Racecourse Lane. David Atkinson was the Mart auctioneer. The Railway Hotel was partially rebuilt. The main line rails form the foreground, with people on them.

The Railway Hotel and Coaching House, 1895. Railway horses were stabled here, behind the archway. The front building was rebuilt in 1902, but the rear building, left, remains. Later it was renamed The Station Hotel to distinguish it from another Railway Inn at North End, near the Stockton Branch.

Otterington, 13 September 1958. The last train to call at this main line station. This and the following sequence of railway photographs were all taken, and comments made, by Jim Sedgwick.

Yafforth gates, 4 september 1955. With "SLS Northern Dales Rail Tour MLS" on the board front and pulling eight coaches, A8 No.69855 and D20 No.62360 begin to gain speed lost by Yafforth Gates' defective down distant signal.

Wiske Moor, 27 September 1955. A water-carrier (a disused tender) which was pushed on to the buffer stops by a goods train had to be re-railed.

Wiske Moor, 13 MAY 1962. The R.C.T.S. (Railway Correspondence and Travel Society) "East Midlander" Rail Tour passes Wiske Moor behind Schools 4-4-0 and LMS 2P.

Wiske Moor, 26 September 1964. The "Great Marquess" and the "Flying Scotsman" overtake a B1 and a diesel shunter at Wiske Moor. Water from the troughs flies up on the right.

Wiske Moor, 26 September 1964. The "Great Marquess" storms over Wiske Moor troughs in a style which would have done credit to a much larger engine. The Gresley syncopated beat was very pronounced indeed! There is an Ian Allan board on the front.

Danby Wiske. The original bridge over the main line at Danby Wiske is here being demolished.

Ainderby, 19 June 1955. The first of two ramblers' specials for Wensleydale pass Ainderby behind 4 MT 2-6-0 No.76020.

Scruton, 20 September 1958. Qb 0-8-0 No.63369 storming through Scruton with a train of mineral empties for Wensley Quarry.

Leeming Bar, 20 September 1958. A Saturday afternoon Horse Box Special passes Leeming Bar on the Wensleydale line.

# Seven

# Farming, and the Family at Brick House Farm

Stooked Cornfield, 1953. The Cleveland Hills form the backdrop. The stooking of corn in the sheaf ended rapidly in the 1950s and early 1960s when combine harvesting took over. (W.C. Fothergill)

Roadside milk stand, 1950s. Mr Ellerby handles the churn. (Dr Owen H. Wicksteed)

Roadside verge, 1950s. Mr Ellerby scythes the grass, and maybe gained some hay.
(Dr Owen H. Wicksteed)

Cleveland bay mare and foal, 1961. This beautiful chestnut breed was the normal workhorse on local farms. Today, with numbers low, they appear on ceremonial occasions, as for example when Mrs J. Parker had Mike Jackson drive Cleveland Bays for her daughter's wedding. In April 1994, at his wish, horse-lover John Cook's body was conveyed from Zion United Reformed Church to Northallerton cemetery in a glass hearse drawn by Cleveland Bays. (Dr Owen H. Wicksteed)

Leading manure. George Bowland, uncle of Mrs Annie Sedgwick of Brick House Farm, Northallerton, farmed at Mill Farm, Swainby and in the Osmotherley area. He was one of eleven children, of whom all the girls died young of T.B. Three or four of the boys lived to be over 90.

Northallerton and District farmers, 26 June 1936. The photograph, with the compliments of Lever Bros. Ltd, records the farmers' visit to Port Sunlight. Edward (Teddy) Doxon, on the far left, Northallerton agent for Lever's cattle food, organised the visit. On the second row, right hand end, is Mrs Parsons, who founded Hutton Bonville WI. Next but one to her, in dark attire, is Mrs Annie Sedgwick. She is still active in 1994 aged 92.

*Opposite above*: Veterinary surgery, 1930s. Vets play an important part in the predominantly farming area around Northallerton. Their former daily lives were related by Thirsk vet Alf Wight in his James Herriot books. Part of the set used by the BBC for filming All Creatures Great and Small was bought by Richmondshire Museum, as seen above.
(Vera Chapman)

*Opposite below*: Yorkshire vets' large animal instruments, 1930s. These are displayed in Richmondshire Museum, Ryders Wynd, Richmond. Above is a horse tube, and below left to right are a humane killer, two dockers and three branding irons. In the case is a preserved trout.
(Vera Chapman)

*Above*: Luke Sedgwick was the great grandfather of Jim Sedgwick, who farms and contracts from Brick House today. Luke was a threshing machine and saw-bench operator who did contract work for farms in the district. He lived at Crakehall House, Crakehall, and died about the time of the First World War in his late 80s.

*Left*: Godfrey Sedgwick packing eggs. Jim's father, Godfrey, kept chiefly Rhode Island Reds.

*Above:* Digging out the car! Jim Sedgwick, Godfrey's son, born in 1935, seemed to revel in the very cold winter of early 1940 (or was it 1941?). He recalls that a special train was needed to lead ice away from the Wiske Moor troughs.

*Right:* Jim Sedgwick with the new tractor. To a young man of 17 or 18, the arrival of the new Ferguson tractor TED diesel of 1953 vintage was an important event. Much later he combined farming with driving one of the four school buses which ferried children in from surrounding farms and villages. He rescued from scrap the fine photograph on page 67 which appears on the cover of this book.

An albion reaper and binder, very early 1950s. Godfrey Sedgwick drives the tractor. The lad near him is Neil Arnott, now a vet.

"Threshing day near Northallerton," 1950s. It is probably at Brick House Farm. (Miss Edna Sedgwick)

Pest control, 1950s. Godfrey Sedgwick loading a gun at Brick House Farm for a necessary duty.

A very wet year. Two tractors were needed to pull a combine harvester in a very wet year at Brick House Farm.

Old and new style barns, September 1963. The coming of machinery, the ousting of horses and the increase in the scale and productivity of farming since the Second World War, meant a revolution also in farm buildings. Small brick and pantile buildings gave way to large span versatile sheds, seen here at the foot of the Cleveland Hills. (Vera Chapman)

Building workers, 1950s. New buildings were erected at Brick House Farm. Left to right: Alf Stead, George Lancaster, Percy Stead (now aged around 90) and Claude Smith.

Concreting the yard. Godfrey and Jim Sedgwick are at the centre.

Northallerton show, September 1949. The Grand Parade was led by Mr R.T. Atkinson of Appleton Wiske with the Best Beast in the Show. (*Ackrill Newspapers* Ltd)

Sheep at Northallerton show, September 1949. The Show is a highlight of the farming year and a social occasion. (*Ackrill Newspapers* Ltd)

*Eight*

# Brompton and Places around Northallerton

Brompton from the church tower. The view is over the green and Shop End towards Cockpit Hill. Water End is beyond.

Brompton village green and Shop End, c. 1897. The old Tollbooth was demolished in 1912.

Brompton in flood at Shop End. Regular floods in Brompton were reputed to be due to a linen mill dam.

ter End, Brompton

Brompton village, water end. The Brompton Beck, or North Beck, winds across the green, and is crossed by fords and small bridges. Note the young trees.

Brompton in flood at water end.

Brompton school group, 1886. Agatha Bradley, born 1882, the girl with the slate, is the grandmother of Mrs Loretta Potter. Next to her, on the right, is Modina Bradley, and between the two is small brother George.

Brompton Whitsun Carnival and sports. This is still a feature of the village on Whit Mondays.

Men workers, Brompton linen mill, 1902. Linen was the chief industry of the village. In 1802 there were eight manufacturers employing around 300 handloom weavers. Later in the nineteenth century the industry was mechanised and concentrated into two mills. Plain and fancy drills, ducks, sheeting and table linen were produced.

Mixed workers group, Brompton linen mill, c. 1902. The lady towards the right with the white bib-front apron is probably the same girl who is holding the slate on page 116.

The Village, Great Smeaton

Village, looking east. The petrol station and garage were demolished for two new houses. The Bay Horse and Black Bull pubs are still there.

Silver Jubilee, May 1935. Great Smeaton celebrates for King George V and Queen Mary with a fancy dress parade and a parade of farm horses. The WI catered for tea and supper, and there were games and a whist drive. Air Commodore Godman's wife, of Smeaton Manor, is on the left with her back to the camera. Captain R.S. Stancliffe's East House is beyond the green.

Village school children, early 1930s. They are outside the old school building, Great Smeaton.

The old school, Great Smeaton. It was replaced by a new building in 1973, and is now a house.

J. Sample calendar, 1883. The picture is entitled "Coming Footsteps". John Sample, Great Smeaton, advertised himself as "Grocer, Tea Dealer and Provision Merchant, N.B. Saddler and Harness Maker".

The Saddlery, Great Smeaton. Little has changed over the years: it is still run by Harry Sample, with his son Billy. Their horse, Topsy, used to graze the village green by St Eloy's church, and pulled Harry's cart when he travelled around to mend harness.

At the great Yorkshire show. Richard (Dick) Lovelace, farmer of Salutation Farm, and Harry Sample, of Great Smeaton Saddlery, enjoy a day out.

Miss Mary Chapman. Harry Sample's fiancée came from Whitburn Colliery in Co. Durham to be the housekeeper at the grocer's shop next door, and became his first wife.

Appleton Wiske, near Great Smeaton. This was a hand-loom weaving village, but is now residential and much renovated and expanded.

The hunt meets at Appleton Wiske. In the background is The Lord Nelson.

East Cowton, 1960s. St Mary's church stood half a mile from the village. A strange mixture of cobbles, stone and brick, with an ancient chancel but an eighteenth-century tower and nave, and curiously furnished, its long history of ill-maintenance culminated in its abandonment in 1910 and ultimately its demolition. The graveyard remains. (Vera Chapman)

East Rounton School, 1975. It was awaiting conversion to a house. Architect Philip Webb, believed to be the inspiration for Bosinny in Galsworthy's Forsyte Saga and an associate of William Morris, designed Rounton Grange in 1872-6 and the school in 1877 for ironmaster Sir Isaac Lowthian Bell. As the school log books record, Lady Bell paid frequent visits in its first year. (Vera Chapman)

Crathorne school group, 1953. Headmistress Miss Clarrie Wetherill. Back row, left to right: David Lowther, Ann Atkinson, Mary Durham, Joy Gibson, Susan Culling, Maurice Calvert, Neil Windspear. Centre row: Peter Alsop, Marion Atkinson, Joan Lawson, Alan Calvert, Sheila Grimston, Helen Hoggarth, Laura Bentley, Glyn Bibson, Mora Cooper, Elizabeth Parsons, Margaret Coates. Front row: Martin Gibson, Ken Vidgen, David Atkinson, Chris Hoggarth, Chris Harston, Joan Coxton, Valerie Dodsworth, Nora Atkinson, Ann Farrow, Eddy Harston, Keith Grimston, Charles Jefferys, Philip Lawson. James, Lord Crathorne, also began his education here "under the eagle eye of Miss Wetherill".

Grange farm bulls, Crathorne, 1944.

*Right*: Maude Violet Dugdale, OBE, JP. The wife of James Lionel Dugdale, she turned Crathorne Hall into a Red Cross Hospital during the First World War, and was its commandant. In the thirteen months from 1914, 222 patients were treated. She is photographed on the steps of The Glade. Her interests covered District Nursing, Education and WIs, and she was the first woman magistrate in Yorkshire. After her son Thomas's election in 1929 as MP for the Richmond Division she was for many years an invalid.

*Below*: Keep fit class, Crathorne, 1930s.

The Holmes, Thirsk. The parish church of St Mary is reflected in a railed-off lake, now a grassed area beside Cod Beck.

Prof. Maurice Beresford, 1963. Author of New Towns of the Middle Ages (1967), he was explaining his theories from the wall of Thirsk parish church. The old settlement at Thirsk continued to flourish, and forms the present market place. The new medieval settlement of St James, set out around a large square beyond the Cod Beck, declined. Curiously today, however, the older settlement near St Mary's church is known as New Thirsk, whilst the later settlement of St James is known as Old Thirsk. (Vera Chapman)

Bedale market place, *c.* 1900. William Pickersgill had the Royal Oak Hotel and Posting House from at least 1890. The Market Cross seems to have been nearer the parish church.

Maypole, Crakehall Show. (Hare of Bedale)

# Acknowledgements

My grateful thanks go to the local people and organisations who allowed me to make copies of their photographs for inclusion in this volume, and gave generously of their time in discussion of the contents:

Mrs Catherine Birch, Geoffrey Clarkson, James Lord Crathorne, William (Billy) Crow, Mr Derbyshire, Mrs G. Vivien Edmunds, the Revd Ian Fox, Mrs Eileen A. Gaskell, Mrs Denny Gibson, Alan Grainger, C.M. (Cassy) Harker, G.K. Hird, B. Holmes, A. Howard, D.W. Jamieson, Ron Jones, J.E. Johnson, Mrs T. Johnston, Mrs Phyllida Joy, E.J. Lewis, K.C. McKeown, Mrs Dorothy Mitchinson, Mrs Ethel Myers, Colin Narramore, Colin New, Mrs J. Parker, the Revd John R. Parker, Mrs Loretta Potter, A. Procter, Peter Richardson, Mrs C. Robinson, Mrs Ella Robinson, Harry Sample, Mrs Annie Sedgwick, J.F. Sedgwick, T.R. Shuttleworth, Alan Suddes, Mrs Marilyn Summers, Mr and Mrs G.J. Swain, Brian Weighell.

Darlington Museum, Northallerton Bowling Club, Northallerton College, Northallerton and District Co-operative Society Ltd, Northallerton Health Services NHS Trust, Northallerton Town Council, The Green Howards Museum, Richmondshire Museum.